KIDS ON EARTH

Wildlife Adventures – Explore The World
Red Fox - Austria

Sensei Paul David

Copyright Page

Kids On Earth: Wildlife Adventures - Explore The World

Red Fox - Austria

by Sensei Paul David,

Copyright © 2023.

All rights reserved.

978-1-77848-189-5 KoE_WildLife_Amazon_eBook_austria_red fox

978-1-77848-188-8 KoE_WildLife_Amazon_eBook_austria_red fox

978-1-77848-424-7 KoE_Wildlife_Ingram_Paperbackbook_RedFox

This book is not authorized for free distribution copying.

www.senseipublishing.com

@senseipublishing
#senseipublishing

Synopsis

This book provides an in-depth look at the Red Fox of Austria. It covers topics such as their behavior, diet, and habitat, as well as their predators and other interesting facts. It also includes information on their protection in Austria and their importance in the Austrian ecosystem. The book is written in an engaging and accessible style and is suitable for children ages 6 to 12.

Get Our FREE Books Now!

kidsonearth.life

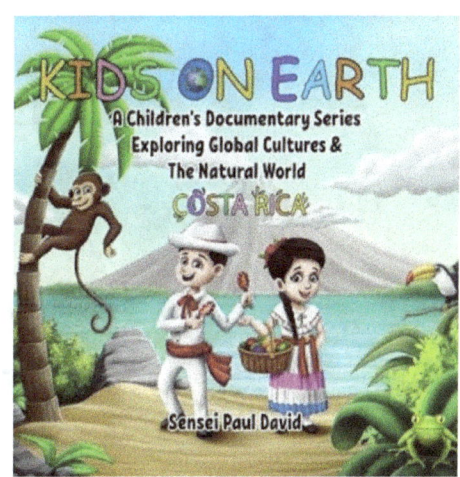

kidsonearth.world

Click Below for Another Book In Each Series

senseipublishing.com/KoE_SERIES

senseipublishing.com/KoE_Wildlife_SERIES

KoE En Español

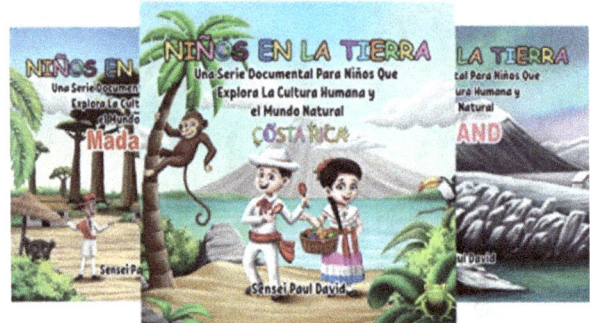

senseipublishing.com/KoE_SERIES_SPANISH

www.senseipublishing.com

Join Our Publishing Journey!

If you would like to receive FUTURE FREE BOOKS and get to know us better, please click www.senseipublishing.com and join our newsletter by entering your email address in the pop-up box.

Follow Our Blog: senseipauldavid.ca

Follow/Like/Subscribe: Facebook, Instagram, YouTube: @senseipublishing

Scan the QR Code with your phone or tablet to follow us on social media:

Like / Subscribe / Follow

Introduction

Welcome to the fascinating world of the Red Fox! Here you will learn about the Red Fox in Austria. They are a beautiful species of fox and are found in all of the Austrian provinces. You will learn about their behavior, diet, and habitat, and all of the amazing things they can do. So let's dive in and learn all about the Red Fox of Austria!

The Red Fox is the largest fox species in Austria.

The Red Fox is also the most widespread fox species in Austria.

Red Foxes are omnivorous, meaning they eat both plants and animals.

Red Foxes are mainly nocturnal, meaning they are most active at night.

The Red Fox's main predators in Austria are the Eurasian Lynx, the Wolf, and the Golden Eagle.

Red Foxes have excellent hearing and can detect prey over long distances.

The Red Fox's coat is usually a rusty red color, but can also be black or silver in some cases.

Red Foxes are social creatures and live in small groups of 3 to 6 individuals.

Red Foxes communicate through a variety of vocalizations, including barks, yelps, and howls.

Red Foxes are usually found in open woodlands or grasslands, but can also be found in urban areas.

Red Foxes are excellent climbers and can climb trees, fences, and walls.

The Red Fox's diet in Austria consists of small mammals, birds, insects, and fruit.

Red Foxes are excellent diggers and can dig burrows for shelter and for storing food.

Red Foxes are monogamous, meaning they mate for life.

Red Foxes can live up to 10 years in the wild and up to 20 years in captivity.

Red Foxes have a gestation period of 51 to 53 days and usually give birth to a litter of 4 to 7 kits.

Red Foxes are very territorial and will defend their territory from intruders.

Red Foxes are very cunning and adapt quickly to their changing environment.

Red Foxes are incredible hunters and can catch prey up to twice their size.

Red Foxes are very intelligent and have been known to play games with each other.

Red Foxes are very vocal and communicate with each other through a variety of calls.

Red Foxes are incredibly agile and can jump up to 3 feet in the air.

Red Foxes are excellent swimmers and can stay underwater for up to 2 minutes.

Red Foxes are curious creatures and often investigate strange noises and smells.

Red Foxes are very curious and will often approach humans if given the opportunity.

Red Foxes are solitary animals and usually hunt alone.

Red Foxes have a good sense of smell and can detect prey up to a mile away.

Red Foxes can be found in all of the Austrian provinces, including Vienna, Salzburg, and Tyrol.

Red Foxes are protected species in Austria and it is illegal to hunt them.

Red Foxes are an important species in the Austrian ecosystem and help to keep the rodent population in check.

Conclusion

The Red Fox of Austria is a fascinating species and deserves to be admired and respected. From their incredible agility and intelligence to their social behavior and diet, they are truly a wonderful species of fox. We hope you have enjoyed learning all about the Red Fox and that this book has inspired you to appreciate and protect this unique species.

Thank you for reading this book!

If you found this book helpful, I would be grateful if you would **post an honest review on Amazon** so this book can reach other supportive readers like you!

All you need to do is digitally flip to the back and leave your review. Or visit amazon.com/author/senseipauldavid click the correct book cover and click on the blue link next to the yellow stars that say, "customer reviews."

As always...

It's a great day to be alive!

Share Our FREE eBooks Now!

kidsonearth.life

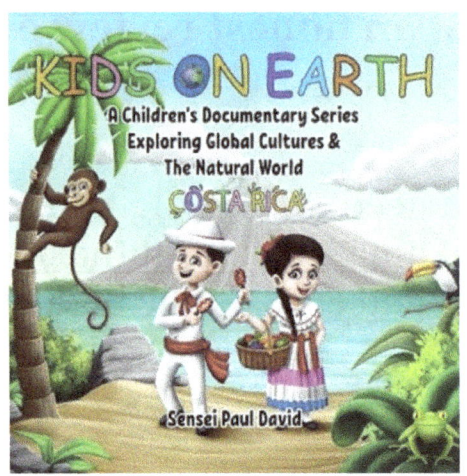

kidsonearth.world

Click Below for Another Book In Each Series

senseipublishing.com/KoE_SERIES

senseipublishing.com/KoE_Wildlife_SERIES

KoE En Español

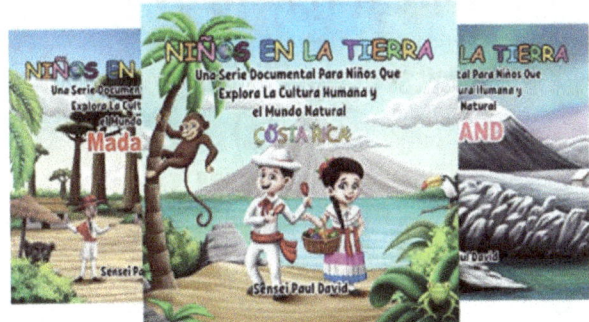

senseipublishing.com/KoE_SERIES_SPANISH

www.senseipublishing.com

www.senseipublishing.com

@senseipublishing
#senseipublishing

Check out our **recommendations** for other books for adults & kids plus other great resources by visiting
www.senseipublishing.com/resources/

Join Our Publishing Journey!

If you would like to receive FREE BOOKS and special offers, please visit www.senseipublishing.com and join our newsletter by entering your email address in the pop-up box

Follow Our Engaging Blog NOW!
senseipauldavid.ca

Get Our FREE Books Today!

Click & Share the Links Below

FREE Kids Books
lifeofbailey.senseipublishing.com
kidsonearth.senseipublishing.com

FREE Self-Development Book

senseiselfdevelopment.senseipublishing.com

FREE BONUS!!!
Experience Over 25 FREE Engaging Guided Meditations!

Prized Skills & Practices for Adults & Kids. Help Restore Deep Sleep, Lower Stress, Improve Posture, Navigate Uncertainty & More.

Download the Free Insight Timer App and click the link below:
<u>http://insig.ht/sensei_paul</u>

About Sensei Publishing

Sensei Publishing commits itself to helping people of all ages transform into better versions of themselves by providing high-quality and research-based self-development books with an emphasis on mental health and guided meditations. Sensei Publishing offers well-written e-books, audiobooks, paperbacks, and online courses that simplify complicated but practical topics in line with its mission to inspire people toward positive transformation.

It's a great day to be alive!

About the Author

I create simple & transformative eBooks & Guided Meditations for Adults & Children proven to help navigate uncertainty, solve niche problems & bring families closer together.

I'm a former finance project manager, private pilot, jiu-jitsu instructor, musician & former University of Toronto Fitness Trainer. I prefer a science-based approach to focus on these & other areas in my life to stay humble & hungry to evolve. I hope you enjoy my work and I'd love to hear your feedback.

- It's a great day to be alive!
Sensei Paul David

Scan & Follow/Like/Subscribe: Facebook, Instagram, YouTube: @senseipublishing

Scan using your phone/iPad camera for Social Media
Visit us at www.senseipublishing.com and sign up for our newsletter to learn more about our exciting books and to experience our FREE Guided Meditations for Kids & Adults.

www.ingramcontent.com/pod-product-compliance
Lightning Source LLC
Chambersburg PA
CBHW080616110526
44587CB00040BB/3731